# Illumination

## A Gnostic Handbook
## For the Post Modern World

Christan Amundsen, M. T.h., M.A.

Sunstar
PUBLISHING LTD.

Illumination
A Gnostic Handbook
United States Copyright, 1998
©Christan Amundsen, M. T.h., M.A.
Sunstar Publishing, Ltd.
207 South 20th Street
Fairfield, Iowa 52556

Cover & Text Design: Amanda Collett

Library of Congress Catalog Card Number: 98-061339
ISBN: 1-887 472-53-3

Readers interested in obtaining further information on the subject
matter of this book are invited to correspond with
The Secretary, Sunstar Publishing, Ltd.
204 South 20th Street, Fairfield, Iowa 52556
More Sunstar Books at www.newagepage.com

# Table of Contents

Preface.................................................. 3

Introduction........................................... 5

The Dilemma......................................... 9

Gnosticism and Christianity.................... 13

We Are Trapped.................................... 16

Freedom Scares Us................................ 20

Something Different................................23

Something More.....................................26

Knowledge.............................................31

The Alien Within....................................35

Gnostic Essentials..................................38

Gnosticism Today...................................65

Appendix A – Atonement Theology.....................68

Appendix B – The Real World............................77

Recommended Reading ..........................82

Glossary.................................................85

## Tears in the Sand
By Christan Amundsen
©1998


I have dropped my tears
in the dry sand of this world.
They are a part of me.
All my life I search for them
like lost children.

Woeful energy lost.
To retrieve myself from the vast dryness
that has absorbed my anguish.
My life collides with others,
who have lost their tears.

This is the way of the world.
The only real water is from
the tears of sorrow shed upon it.
Life itself has come from it,
and to it, life must return.

I cannot stay here long.
But to leave I must redeem my tears.
I have dropped them in the dry sand.
All my life I search for them
like lost children.

*...that which you have will save you
if you bring it forth from yourselves.
That which you do not have within you [will] kill you
if you do not have it within you."*

-The Gospel of Thomas vs. 70-

## Preface

The purpose of this book is to provide an introduction to Post-Modern Gnosticism. It is not meant to be an exhaustive study of the topic. It is only a starting place-an attempt to offer an explanation of Gnosticism in an accessible manner. The word "gnostic" means: one who knows or one who has familiarity. A Gnostic is one who holds a special knowledge or awareness. In pursuit of this knowledge one seeks the answer to one essential question: Who am I? This question seems simple at first glance, but once pondered, the seeker learns that the answer provides the key to the very question of existence itself. A realization that the gnostic path has many difficulties is the beginning place. Knowledge comes at a personal cost but it is truly a treasure that cannot be stolen or decay. Comparing Gnosticism to the many dying, authoritarian belief systems that exist is like comparing light to darkness.

Gnosticism has two primary sources - direct experience of being a human being, and revealed knowledge about our spiritual origin. Both are the subject of this book. These two sources converge to form an understanding of who we are, why we are here and where we are. Gnosticism pushes deeply into the knowledge of our own experience of self and world. It is akin to existentialism, in that it takes very seriously our feelings about our lives and the discomfort of being human. This knowledge is direct for all of us - we can know it without faith in a doctrine or religious dogma. Much of this book will deal with our direct experience, since it is foundational to gnostic understanding. Revealed knowledge also falls within experience, but it requires a great deal more effort to explain. This is so primarily because of the nature of the world itself, which has a sort of "noise" that clouds our hearing of anything alien to it. Without access to revealed knowledge we are left with some overwhelming dilemmas regarding the basic questions of our being. Through the convergence of our direct experience and revealed wisdom we form a body of knowledge we call "gnosis".

This book is a starting point. The beginner may see the approach as strange or unusual. Gnostics tend to be rather plain spoken on certain issues, while on other ideas the discussion becomes more mytho-poetic. *The key thing for the seeker is this: abandon your preconceived ideas and open your mind to that which you already know deep inside your true self. Find the truth of your own experience, and be present with it from a clear perspective. Allow yourself to seek insight deep within and listen to "The Calling" that comes from something higher and separate from the ordinary reality of the world. That which is revealed to you and that which you already know will unify. That unification is the awareness you seek. It is the saving gnosis.*

## Introduction

*"I am the hearing that is attainable to everything;
I am speech that cannot be grasped"*

-The Thunder, Perfect Mind

*"As he went on his way Jesus saw a man blind from his birth. His disciples put the question, 'Teacher, who sinned, this man or his parents?' Why was he born blind?' 'It is not that this man or his parents sinned', Jesus answered; 'he was born blind so that God's power might be displayed in curing him. While daylight lasts we must carry on the work of him who sent me; night comes when no one can work. While I am in the world I am the light of the world.'"*

-John 9: 1-5

Read this story carefully. Jesus says, "it is not that this man sinned or his parents" - his blindness is not related to sin but to the nature of his birth. Jesus is saying that life is that way. We are born into blindness, not sin. We are born to an unseeing captivity. This captivity is not caused by any sinful nature, but by the nature of this world. Because it is the nature of this world to have caused a man to be blind for no other reason than his birth alone, it can also reveal the power and distinction between a loving God and the natural course of the world. Thus the world causes us to be blinded to something higher and deeper about ourselves.

This story, like so many others, is a metaphor. A metaphor for what it means to live in this world. Taking this story as a metaphor allows us to see that to be born at all is to be blinded into a kind of unconsciousness that narrows our reality and chokes our spirit. It is not sin that we must be redeemed from, we must be redeemed from our unconsciousness. That was Jesus' message.

How did this message of liberation from unconsciousness become the kind of Christianity we see and hear about today? How did the message become about obedience and blind faith, when the real message was about being found and awakened to the existence of the true self.

Jesus was not an orthodox thinker. He criticized the religious thinking of his day. He called the religious leaders "blind guides" who set up barriers to people. These rules and regulations kept folks unconscious and under the spell of religious and political authority. Jesus was about revealing people to themselves—being a light to those living in darkness, as the scriptures put it.

Somewhere Jesus' message got lost. He died as a result of awakening people. His ideas shook the very foundations of religious and societal thought. Later, his so called followers replaced Jesus' message of the struggle for freedom and awareness with a religious system of atonement for sin. Old ideas were repackaged, describing God as angry and jealous about human behavior. Defined by the prevailing authorities of the time, the old ideas became a new religion.

There is a sadness felt by most spiritual people to greater or lesser degrees. This sadness is caused by the fact that the message of truth and freedom is denied by most churches. The message is only carried by a precious few—the thinkers and mystics, mostly exiled to universities or removed from the church altogether. A great theologian, who I once studied under, once told me that he felt as if he had no church he could attend. He had stopped attending church altogether. This troubled him greatly, but the message that he understood to be central to the church's existence was not there. He found it only among the struggling questions of his students.

Perhaps Christianity died the day that it became the religion of the Empire under Constantine, and has been in a process of decay ever since. Freedom from the terrorism and oppression of this world became obedience to the Emperor, and adherence to the laws of the state. Perhaps it was the failure of thinkers such as Augustine, who turned away from his more Gnostic beginnings to frame an emphasis on human sin—arguing that human beings were not capable of ruling themselves. Perhaps it was just the times itself. To be sure the argument that humans are slaves to sin is understandable. Evil and injustice abound and

7

so many seem willing partners to such actions. Perhaps the answer is not so much that human beings are slaves to sin, but merely that humans are slaves and as a result of that slavery we begin to feel and act destructively as the captivity itself dictates. It comes as no surprise that the gnostics would say that creation is not all that good, and that human beings are not all that free.

It stands to reason that one might begin to think, as Carl Jung did in his "Answer to Job", that God had created the world without consulting His own wisdom. Perhaps God had essentially created the world out of his own unconsciousness, and is in the process Himself of becoming aware; a kind of divine evolution that parallels our own. Perhaps there is a dualistic aspect to the created order, in which a lesser God was involved in the creation of the world (as Gnostics believed). Most of the church since Constantine chose to believe that human beings are at fault—having fallen from obedience to God by choice, making freedom the problem not the answer. We see the intense opposition of ideas; a struggle that has gone on for centuries.

We are at a unique time in history. Church power is waning—people don't fear the "wrath of God' as much anymore. Many people walk away from any form of spirituality altogether. Sadly, there are societal forces that keep people unconscious as well. Hopefully this book will offer encouragement for the seeker and an opportunity to better understand who we are.

## The Dilemma

"...and do not do what you hate, for all
things are plain in the sight of heaven. For nothing
hidden will not become manifest, and nothing
covered will remain without being uncovered"

-The Gospel of Thomas, vs. 6

Bringing someone out of denial and unconscious living is much more difficult than merely correcting behavior and maintaining a construct of belief and ritual. One might behave and conform, and yet remain unaware and ignorant. The vast majority of people choose a religious path that does not emphasize awareness, knowledge and freedom. Most choose, as a kind of standard path, a blind faith that substitutes thinking and authentic consciousness with dogmatic and rigid belief systems. These systems literalize myth and suppress dynamic expression of the spirit. Fundamentalism has used the Bible to cause even greater suffering and further obscure the deep truths that exist. We remain blind because we are not pushed to open our eyes and our minds. Most people are taught to make a deal with God. The deal goes like this: If you buy into the orthodox religious system that requires certain actions, believe the simple answers as taught, and obey the rules given—God will be happy with you. This deal excludes the hard inner work required by authentic, conscious living. You uphold the deal by being good, acting according to the rules, and by having good "traditional values". Believe in God, and you'll be fine. Right?

Wrong! We aren't fine because we are left just as ignorant as before. Worse still we are taught to fear deep spiritual questioning because it may upset people. Also feared is the wrath of God—a divine sort of "Thought Police" that will attack us for having the audacity to ask, "why?" So the majority plods on, Zombie like, in a sort of trance—unaware.

Elaine Pagels, in her wonderful book titled: *The Gnostic Gospels*, quotes the Gnostic Gospel of Valentinus, *The Gospel of Truth*, as saying:

"...ignorance...brought about anguish and terror. And the anguish grew solid like a fog, so that no one was able to see. For this reason error is powerful..."

10

She writes, "Most people live, then, in oblivion - or in contemporary terms, in unconsciousness. Remaining unaware of their true selves, they have 'no root'. The Gospel of Truth describes such existence as a nightmare." She continues, "Those who live in it experience 'terror and confusion and instability and doubt and division', being caught in 'many illusions'. So according to the passage scholars call the Nightmare Parable, they live:

– as if they were sunk in sleep and found themselves in disturbing dreams. Either (there is )a place to which they are fleeing, or without strength, they come (from) having chased after others, or they are involved in striking blows, or they are receiving blows themselves, or they have fallen from high places...When those who are going through all these things wake up, they see nothing...for they are nothing. Such is the way of those who have cast ignorance aside as sleep, leaving (its works) behind like a dream in the night...This is the way everyone has acted, as though asleep at the time when he was ignorant. And this is the way he has come to knowledge, as if he had awakened. (p. 125)

This Nightmare Parable describes perfectly the people of our time - living in a kind of sleep, and accepting the terrible reality being created over and over again by our own darkness. Within this nightmare, knowledge and consciousness become suspect. People fear, to varying degrees, the educated, enlightened and knowledgeable because the Nightmare has become the norm. Anyone who challenges that reality is called a heretic or radical.

The issue central to this dilemma is the truth that we are living in a false reality; a reality that is bound by religions and institutions whose job it is to maintain the status quo. Christianity took a wrong turn when it placed doctrines, rituals, sin and atonement as centrally important. Awakening and knowledge were abandoned as dangerous. Blind faith replaced real faith. Real faith only exists as long as it seeks knowledge and truth. Blind faith requires acceptance of external authority that demands strict obedience. History shows countless acts of destruction committed in the name of God. These people had lots of blind faith, but never awakened to the truth and so became instruments of darkness.

It is easy to stop seeking and become a passive, cog in the machine, pawn. How easy it is to stay asleep, not seeking truth and freedom, desiring only to lay back and have another's will replace the uncomfortable work of true spirituality.

If one thing is clear it is this there must be a great struggle from the ignorance that holds us in bondage.

Obedience to God must follow the truth of God and the freedom to discover that truth with conscious awareness. Christianity has all too often placed the cart before the horse by making doctrine and self recrimination more important than the search for truth and freedom. The proof of this lies in the fact that after almost 1700 years of orthodox Christianity, nothing spiritually essential has changed for humanity, and the majority remains blind and ignorant.

# Gnosticism and Christianity

"...is it something from heaven or
is it something from earth?"

-The Dialogue of the Savior, vs. 88

The relationship between Gnosticism and Christianity is difficult to describe. The last 1700 years of organized religion has obscured the truth. Atonement theology (See Appendix I) replaced self awareness and self-knowledge with self recrimination. The desire for power and control replaced the desire for enlightenment.

Gnosticism is real Christianity and vice versa. Both are a context in which to journey through life. True Christianity is metaphor and story; its truths are seen through the windows of its stories—not in the literalization of them. I think it is important for the Gnostic to save the stories of Christianity. The truths contained must be saved from the onslaught of ignorance and error that is the real problem, the real definition of "sin". The ignorance and error seen within all religious traditions is but an expression and error we live in about ourselves. Christianity was meant to be a spirituality about making the unconscious conscious, about freeing people from inner slavery and psychic oppression. For Jesus and the Gnostics, it was a spirituality about recovery of self, and finding a new sense of being in the world. It is tragic that the name "Christian" no longer carries its true meaning.

Salvaging the truth from the muck of ignorance is much like panning for gold—much work is required, but finding the treasure makes the effort relatively insignificant. Christianity began among the discontent of society, among those who had not fared well with rules and mores. Christianity was an outlaw religion—an outlaw spiritual sense of the world.

The truths brought forth by Christianity shattered the spiritual malaise of the first few centuries A.D.. After years of persecution, it became apparent that Christianity could not be destroyed. A split occurred when one group of Christian leaders attempted to set up an authoritative system, shifting the focus to earthy power rather than pushing toward inner knowledge. The orthodox clergy became polarized against the Gnostics. Orthodoxy began to use earthly power, politics and authority to control the beliefs of early Christians in order to keep ideas "pure". Political power prevailed and the Gnostics were banished to obscurity—for a time.

Gnosticism is a perspective of dissatisfaction with the world. Those who are Gnostics have an intense sense of their own alienation from the world. Wherever there is a spirit of maintaining the status quo or talk of returning to "better times" of the past, Gnosticism always stands in opposition. Because Gnosticism is a perspective that must always be lived on the edge, it is never a comfortable religion.

Gnosticism requires the hard inner work of seeing the "oblivion" or unconsciousness of our living. It requires us to strip away denial and illusion in order to find our true selves. Complacency is antithetical to Gnosis.. You cannot serve two masters, you cannot gain real enlightenment without losing your false self. You cannot hang on to abuse, hurt and the poverty of passive living and enter a different kind of reality, called by Jesus: "The Kingdom of God".

This is where Gnosticism begins. It is not a "let's all be good little boys and girls" religion nor does it offer a simplistic set of rules and regulations to follow. It is about liberation and self knowledge. It relates to the interior of human beings and impacts the exterior of our political, social and economic realities. Gnosticism brings with it a dynamic force that pushes us toward new and deeper understandings of self and the universe.

## We Are Trapped

*" ...by his acts and acquaintance each
person will make his nature known."*

-On the Origin of the World, vs. 127:15

John is a man who has come to me for therapy. He is miserable by his own account. He feels a slave to his wife, his job and his responsibilities. He says of himself, "I've done everything right in my life. I've always been the good guy - dependable and stable. I always thought that if I did what I was told, and did all the right things, my life would be happy. Well, I'm not happy— I'm miserable."

I've told John that his misery is not an enemy. Actually his misery is his friend, for behind his misery is a great truth, one that he needs to hear. He does not need to be "cured" from his misery and depression, he needs to walk through it, and discover the truth of it. John squirms in his chair when we talk about reclaiming his life. He knows that it will cost him the comfort of his complacency. At 50 years old John is no longer totally asleep. He's not fully awake yet to who he is or what his life means, but he's no longer a willing slave to the kind of sleep and intoxication that conformity to society brings. John wants out. No one is really persecuting John, but inside John feels persecuted; trapped and enslaved. He has possessions, lots and lots of "things"; everything he could think of to try to fill the void in his life.

John's misery is his greatest friend. It does not feel good, but truth rarely does. He is sitting amongst his hopelessness, and now he has no energy left to run. When I look out at the world I see it filled with people like John. John is Kierkegaard's "Philistine" - one who "tranquilizes itself with the trivial". He, like the masses of people, are "shut-up". John now has to dispel the inner lie that has guided him throughout his life. "There must be more than this" John laments. Somewhere, deep inside, the dim spark of his soul knows that there is more—much more than he can possibly imagine at this time.

John's salvation lies in his awakening to a new self-knowledge. That new self-knowledge can move him to find a sense of freedom. His intuitive self-knowledge began the process - as the ancient Gnostics said it would. By listening to this knowledge, John begins to walk toward a deeper sense of his real being. It is an initiation into the inner regions; the path to one's true Home.

In verse 69 of the Gospel of Thomas, Jesus says: "blessed are they who have been persecuted within themselves. It is they who have truly come to know God." Those of us who have come to know this inner persecution have an opportunity to discover the true God—the reality behind this world of shadows. The true God calls to us, and until we listen we never discover our true selves or real freedom.

Salvation is the process of finding our true selves and our true Home. It is always worked out within the context of "fear and trembling", because it is about listening to that voice of truth. That voice finally tells us that this world has lied to us, and that all the promises of culture, family and money have nothing whatsoever to do with the real stuff that makes us who we are. As the early Gnostics learned, the world is not all that good, and we are not all that free. But, we can find purposefulness within the darkness of the world. Awareness of the darkness can reveal our true self which has its reality beyond the hurtfulness of this life.

The ancient Gnostic traditions spoke of the human predicament as being ignorance, sleep, intoxication, and forgetfulness. Trapped in ignorance is the true "fallen" character of being human - it is the real "sin" we live out in our lives. It is this ignorance or intoxication from which we must awaken if we are to discover our real self and a pathway out of the unconscious sleep we have slipped into. As a metaphor, this unconsciousness of our true being is like the medallion placed around the necks of ancient slaves. These slaves literally wore the name of their masters. Consciousness of true self requires a kind of radical disobedience to the old master—a revolution that occurs first within, and then reveals itself as an awakened life. Like the slaves of old, that scratched the name of the redeemer on the flip side of his slave disc as a statement of a new identity — he moved outside earthly law.  No longer a slave to the old self, the former slave finds freedom and cannot be threatened by physical death.  The slave passes over from the death of unconsciousness into the life of knowledge about his true self.

We are trapped.  That is a fundamental of Gnosticism. To be a human is to be lost in a kind of unconsciousness that requires an awakening.  We can look upon our inner disturbances as inner stirrings of that spirit that longs for freedom and a voice.

## Freedom Scares Us

*"...let him who seeks continue seeking
until he finds. When he finds, he will
become troubled"*

-The Gospel of Thomas, vs 2

Obsession, in whatever form - alcoholism, drug addiction, consumerism, rage, sexual or romantic, is a response to our inner sense of being trapped. Obsession is meant to alleviate the anxiety of our intuition by narrowing the focus of life into a small, manageable event or practice. It is a way we try to cope with our slavery, not by freeing ourselves, but by changing the nature of the slavery into something else; a kind of rebellion without a jail break. Not only are we trapped in ignorance, we fear the knowledge that might set us free, and we fear any movement toward that freedom. Obsession is the way we maintain our slavery, but deny it is there. Our primary obsession is the socio-economic systems in which all of us live. It is our collective obsession. We hate it, yet we fear being without it. We become slaves to the marketplace, and the more effective we are at manipulating this obsession, the more we can deny our ignorance of self, and simply praise ourselves for our so-called riches. Jesus pegged it when he said, "you cannot worship two masters - God and money." Our society has created the collective obsession as a way to divorce ourselves from the reality of the suffering and pain of our false self and existence. We make ourselves comfortable, and our comfort keeps us afraid of our freedom. The poor are blessed, not because it feels good to be poor, or that poverty has virtue, but because being poor reveals how dark this world is, and how it taints our soul with intoxication concerning the starkness of real life in the material world. To place your value on materialism rather than spirituality is to be poor in the world of the spirit, and to focus on a spiritual life is to be rich in the spirit. This is not to say that being rich is bad and being poor is good. Where you place your value is most important. You cannot buy spirituality and inner peace. Rich or poor, we all must do the hard work of inner spirituality to find our true selves amongst society's distractions. That was the message of Jesus with regard to the obsession of the economic order. To strip away comfort was the work of the redeemer, because it laid bare the obsession and jarred people awake.

Being awakened and becoming free scares us. Freedom

and self-knowledge are uncomfortable, and make us aware of how oppressive and alien the world is. It's easier to stay asleep and a slave. Asleep, we don't have to make decisions, and can easily blame others for anything bad that happens to us, because, after all, we aren't in charge. So freedom scares us, and we flee it by convincing ourselves that we can't leave our obsession or our "situation".

African slaves were brought to this country against their will and forced to serve their white masters. They were, for the most part, kept in slavery not by chains, but through fear and the idea that escape was impossible. They were told that to run away would be certain death, that they would starve or the wild animals or Indians would get them. The modern form of slavery is this type of thinking: "I can't leave this job I hate because I'll lose my benefits." Or, "I can't leave this abusive marriage because I can't make it on my own." More commonly, "I can't possibly go against what I've been taught my whole life." This is slavery indeed, and yet we have a kind of perverse comfort with it. We get to "play" the martyr, and our martyrdom enables us to avoid the anxiety of freedom and authenticity.

Gnosticism always takes a contra-position to this kind of self-imposed martyrdom and ritual self - abuse. That is why Gnosticism is so difficult to live with—it requires us to be free, and walk through our fear of being genuine. It requires us to wake up and find out who we really are, regardless of our fears.

## Something Different

*"...blessed is the soul of those men
because they have known God with a knowledge
of the truth! They shall live forever..."*

-The Apocalypse of Adam, vs. 83

Salvation is basically the willingness to know something different about ourselves and the world other than what we are programmed with. The "Kingdom of God" that Jesus speaks of has a foot in two spheres - the world of the soul and the world of the spirit.

The soul sphere is the stuff of our contact with this world and its meaning for us. Our soul stuff is the world of our heart, and our longing to literally touch the material around us and form something of it. In a real sense we create our soul. We build it and nurture it, or we deny it and destroy it. It is the inner seed that either grows into the strong inner life that it longs to be, or gets no fertilizer and just sits there. Soul stuff is always heavy stuff. It literally weighs upon us, and our times of soul making are always very difficult times. Growth of soul has to push its way through the dirt and mud to reach light and water. Our soul is at home here in this world, because it is of this world. It does its work here.

The sphere of the spirit is different. It does not come from this material. Its real existence is from beyond the conscious ego world, and lives in the realm behind, above and even under all things. It cannot be touched, nor seen, and cannot be spoken of directly as one might speak of an object. The spirit "visits" the material world. It is light, as the ancients called it. It is in this world of the spirit, that we are most blind. Our birth into the world of matter and concrete existence makes this world of spirit only a dream; a shadow dance from the backdrop of light. To sense it, one dives deep into the unconscious life of being itself. We begin to honor dreams and visions, and in a profound kind of way, begin the process of turning reality on its end. We begin to see that our identification with our ego self is a kind of obsession which only detracts and even denies the deeper reality of a world underneath and above all things.

Unlike soul-making, which concerns itself with issues of

24

meaning, the world of the spirit has as its concern experience itself. Experience which, as in most things, has a kind of strength and weakness to it. Obsession becomes possible through the concern of experience, and hence the character of being a lost spirit comes with a spirit being trapped by its own concern for experience. Release, as the ancient Gnostics thought, comes when our self-knowledge begins to transcend our obsessions. Our obsessions are overcome through our soul-making, which is why the two spheres are so linked together. Our soul-making creates a thirst for meaning and purpose. It touches upon our obsessions with our over identified ego existence, soul-making begins the process of seeking the world of the spirit, and as the two unite, a kind of knowledge, or gnosis, occurs that can only be called an awakening.

The cornerstone of Gnosticism is awakening from the blindness of our obsessions. The Gnostic finds the true sense of ourselves that releases us from the bondage to the one dimensional life that plagues our existence. Gnosticism will be rediscovered in that area of discipline between psychology and religion - where the sphere of soul meets the sphere of the spirit. The place where meaning collides with experience, and where obsession is turned into self-knowledge. It will find discovery by those who are not so firmly rooted in the socioeconomic structures that are our primary obsessions. Gnosticism will always be discovered by those who have to discover a different way - something more than merely existing in an unjust world.

## Something More

*"...and he blew into his face the spirit
which is the power of his mother; he did not
know (this), for he exists in ignorance..."*

-The Apocalypse of John, vs 19

Gnosticism is about a presence of something within us that is of a profoundly fuller reality than the reality of the natural process.

One reason why Human Beings feel so alienated from each other is that something within reveals a distancing effect from living in the material world. We are conscious of how the material world separates us from each other, and builds boundaries that don't exist within the context of being itself. Like lines between countries that appear on a flat map, boundary lines do not exist when seen from the reality of observation in the world. This experience begins the journey into seeing self apart from the dictates of the material form of the world. Reflections of this profoundly different reality exist within the context of our loving relationships and our ability to think abstractly about qualities that have a spiritual significance to us, but have no concrete existence in the natural world. We might call this abstract reality or supranatural reality - because it exists within us, and not within natural process of the empirical order of things. The Ten Commandments, for example, are said to be "divinely" imparted, because they cannot be inferred by the natural processes of the world. They appear within, and not from without. The point is that this law or supranatural morality is a product of something greater than the world, and this production of supranatural reality creates a kind of religious instinct in Human Beings that further points to a reality beyond the scope of mere material reality.

We begin to see the difference between something in ourselves and the natural order. We see the difference between what it means to be consciousness driven and instinct driven. Although we feel both, it is our awareness of the "higher self" that divides us from the mindless process of materiality.

"What will a man gain by winning the whole world at the

cost of his true self?" (Matt. 16:26). This is a spiritual theme
running through much of the New Testament, and certainly
through the Gnostic Scriptures. In the Gospel of Thomas, Jesus
observes: "I am amazed at how this great wealth (true self) has
come to dwell in this poverty" (vs.29). The poverty that Jesus
speaks of is this world - the world of material reality, and the world
of the social order of human beings that was created by us to
protect ourselves from the harshness of that natural reality. In
essence, everything "of this world" is a kind of poverty that
darkens the true self - keeps it drunk, as it were. It is not until we
are loosened from this world that our true self can be revealed.
What I have seen with alcoholics and drug addicts is that their
addictions, which are their undoing, are also their salvation. Their
poverty leads to the addiction, which forces them to a point of
ultimate decision, a deep kind of spiritual crisis, which leads into
an experience of "higher power" that liberates and brings "sanity."
It is a loosening process that frees the spirit into self-knowledge.
AA and other recovery groups are good quasi Gnostic forms.
They start with powerlessness, and end with spiritual awakening.

But seeing that our inner reality is different from the
external reality of the material and social world is just the first step
of freeing ourselves. If we follow that difference it brings us to the
awakening that the "something different" inside is also higher and
deeper, more lasting and certainly more loving. Eventually, if the
AA/addict does the inner work, he comes to see that this inner
reality is true, and all the external stuff is but an error, or a kind of
darkness. The experience that our dark side lives on the outside
not on the inside is a huge revelation. We are so programmed to
think that we are the darkness, that everything becomes turned
around. We stand on our heads. The light within trapped by the
darkness of the external world begins to delude itself that the
darkness is a reflection of its own inner reality - and the self hatred
begins. That is how we learn to live in this great poverty.

We begin to live in this "great poverty" through a kind of
hardening process. Our consciousness of "true self" becomes so

covered over and encased by external reality, that it appears to us not to exist at all. Children are taught to obey authority and undergo a process of dissolving their spirituality - that is, their ability to literally see the world differently from the hardened reality of their parents and society. Reality becomes so narrowly defined that it can be called "poverty". Spirituality gets reduced to either doctrinal religion, or being a "good person." Neither idea has much to do with the larger issue of finding one's "true self" that is locked within a hardened sense of reality. The body, or the world, both become metaphors for this hardened reality sense in Gnostic literature: It is true poverty.

The mask of this hardened reality makes us sweat. It is uncomfortable. We begin to see a difference between an inner sense of love and compassion, and the external world of harsh reality - both natural and social. This conflict causes a sort of psychic heat. If we sweat enough, we begin to sense that our inner reality is a "true self" much more than any externalized sense of self given to us by family, friends or society.

At the center of Gnosticism is the reality that human beings are alienated from the world in which they find themselves. This is not speculative philosophy, it is an existential reality - a reality that each of us has in common. It has psychological ramifications, such as anxiety, depression, violence and many other features, as well as psychological defense mechanisms such as denial, obsessive compulsive behavior, and many other characteristics. On the topic of alienation most thinkers would agree to some degree. When it comes to the "why" of this alienation there is broad disagreement.

Alienation, from conventional perspectives, is an indication that something is wrong with the individual, whether it is a sign of sin, a character flaw or a neurosis. But from the Gnostic orientation, this alienation is the first indication that something is right with the individual. Gnosticism argues that alienation itself is part of the fundamental structure of material existence, and is not simply a character flaw, sin or lack of faith. It is a kind of prison that humans are enslaved in that keeps them away from the knowledge of their true being which is abstract and spiritual. In Gnostic literature, the world is called "darkness", because it is the place of imprisonment of the spirit. Release occurs through knowledge of true self, which enables the individual to unlock the attachment from unconscious and invisible forces that keep them in slavery to the material world. When a person begins the process of discovery of their true self, which is a spiritual quality, it is a kind of realized resurrection, or as it is sometimes called, being "born again."

This awakening from the "darkness" of the world into the "light" of true self is salvation from the Gnostic perspective. This awakening releases the individual from fixation on the world as the ultimate authority, or ultimate reality. In fact, the material world becomes a kind of secondary reality that ceases to have the impact once felt when the person was unconscious of their true self. This loosening of attachment from the force of the material world enables a kind of serenity of life, because the individual no longer ascribes power to it, realizing that within each of us is a power greater than the world. That is why Jesus would say with great authority, "I am in the world, but not of it."

The core issue in Gnosticism is not redemption from sin, but salvation from ignorance and unconsciousness. Gnosticism demands, therefore, not belief and contrition, but spiritual effort and diligence. Without this effort and diligence, people are literally lost in unaware living, and unconscious forces rule their very existence. To be aware - to know one's True Self - is to know God. That is the saving gnosis.

## Knowledge

*"...bring in your guide and your teacher.*
*The mind is the guide, but reason is the teacher.*
*They will bring you out of destruction*
*and dangers."*

-The Teachings of Silvanus, VII, 85

Within Gnosticism there are primarily two sources of knowledge. The first we would now term existential knowledge, or experience of the world. This is not speculative philosophy or conjecture, but facts of existence. And what are the facts of existence? First, that the defining characteristic of life is process, with death as the final outcome. In this way, material existence holds within itself self-nullification. In the face of this outcome, human beings who are conscious of death as a threat to their person hood, create psychological and social defenses. They also create a kind of intensity to life - anxiety, fearfulness, hope, longing and a host of human values that have a cutting edge of negativity to them, yet find their way into the forefront in all that we do and share.

Perhaps one of the most important aspects of this existential knowledge is that life itself is meaningless - which is to say, that meaning is an internal human notion, not an objective external thing to be measured and studied. To live life amidst this kind of emptiness, driven by our own internal senses to project meaning and value upon external form, is all part of the human struggle and dilemma. Try as we may, we feel empty here, because it is empty. The vastness and awesome nature of physical reality is terrifying without reason and purpose, and thus we move quickly to fill the void with all the projected power of our psyches - which are fundamentally a part of the process as well. And as we see the connection between our psychological self and the world around us, the more shocked we become. We become either driven inside ourselves for deeper answers, or we flee to desperate acts of trying to comfort ourselves with food, technology, romance, politics, money or any number of things that we as humans surround ourselves with.

To stand back and look at ourselves is a most difficult thing. It never feels good. We see how everything has affected us and taught us to think the way we think, or to act the way we act. Our parents, schools, institutions of religion and government, all are a part of a common reality or sense that in every way divorces us from the truth of who we really are. We are buried underneath layers of "stuff" and sentimental ideas. The deepest existential truth is that we are lost - lost amidst the world where we feel alien and anxious, forlorn and homesick. We want to know "why?" This we never quite glean from all the things of the world, until somehow we are broken and rise up to escape our imprisonment.

At some point, and only we know when that point is and how it comes, we give up. Nothing seems to help. If we are honest with ourselves, and not driven back into the mindless seeking of comfort through the things of the world. We just surrender. At that moment, and perhaps only at that moment, can we hear the voice of something more within ourselves calling, as it were, to a higher reality of self. A reality that drives us toward a "Home" from which that self belongs. It is knowledge that does not come from this world - the world of form and material reality. It comes from some alien, non-spatial place which for the most part is indescribable. It is revealed, not found through objective inquiry. It is presented, not discovered through research. It is.

This is the second source of Gnostic knowledge: Revelation. This revelation is not from some creator God who speaks within the material process, but from a God of truth beyond all space, time, matter and energy. Revelation speaks to that which belongs to it - the spirit, or spark. It cannot be measured, and it cannot be observed. It is not heard in any way one might judge hearing, nor is it felt in any way one might judge feeling. It simply awakens the innermost core of us that was before all things; before the sleep of existence came upon us. It is light into darkness.

When one awakens to this revelation, the false self of material and psychological reality begins to fade as if consumed by some magical fire. The awakening can be slow or fast, for the layers of sleep are many, and the forces of darkness are deep. With this awakening one begins to live within its presence, and not in the world at all. It is as Jesus said, "I am in the world, but not of it." The existential knowledge becomes mitigated by the

33

revelation, and the false reality of the material world begins to lose its power.

## The Alien Within

*"I am... within."*

-The Thunder, Perfect Mind

Living beneath our physical and mental features is an alien being which we commonly refer to as the "spirit". So often in our language we misunderstand just how alien this spirit is, because we tend to speak of it in terms that are not alien at all, such as "energy". Energy is, to be sure, a secondary category or resultant aspect of spirit, as is materiality. But it is not one and the same, nor can speaking of an energy force be construed as the same as the spirit. The spirit is wholly other than any and all aspects of the universe of matter and energy, although it in part resides, if you can speak of it residing, within us and in all life to some degree. Life could not be life without it, and in a sense life can be said to use the spirit to be what it is, namely, something animate.

This alien within us is a captive of the universe of material and energy. The universe did not create it, nor does it sustain it. In fact, the universe could not be animate at all without this alien spirit. This alien spirit is enslaved to the material and energy world, precisely because it is lost amidst the fog of substance. The spirit, then, indirectly and unwittingly becomes a part of the universe, and life begins. Life could not come about without this alien reality. To say, therefore, that the Spirit is evolving is not precise, since the alien spirit itself is not in process but simply animates the evolution of life through its own entrapment.

Before the universe was, the Spirit or "All" was. The alien that resides within us, is a fragment or spark of that alien and divine spirit. It is trapped here in a kind of spiritual slumber. Apart from spirit, the universe could not live, which is to say, that it would cease. When all the sparks of this alien spirit depart from the material and energy forms in which it is trapped, the universe will cease to be alive - and will become once again the formless void that it was and truly is.

Death and all the processes of the universe are alien to the spirit - the true self. Thereby life can be said to be a kind of illusion, because it is an interplay of light and shadow that confuses and keeps the alien lost. Buried deep within the material process of biology and psyche, the spirit gives life through its sleep, but upon awakening begins the process of loosening itself from the stranglehold of material existence. Without this awakening, the alien remains in the state of slumber, and continues to tumble within the process of the universe, kept within an alien world, giving life to it through its own enslavement. Spiritual awakening does not propel one toward suicide as one might imagine with this understanding. Quite the contrary, suicide in and of itself does nothing to release the spirit from the material force of the universe. Suicide may merely be anger that keeps the spirit attached to the form it seeks to repel against. Dying to the world on the spiritual level is quite different. It is a withdrawal from finding primary meaning and purpose in material substance, and ceasing to be enchanted by the tumbling and ever changing shapes of the material world. This withdrawal does not require one to depart from society or live apart from others, although one might choose to do so. It is an act of inward change, where the spirit becomes truly aware of itself, and begins to seek its true home beyond the scope of the universe.

## Gnostic Essentials

*"He does not see through the soul nor through the spirit, but the mind which [is] between the two..."*

-The Gospel of Mary

Underneath all Gnostic thought are some essential perspectives. These perspectives, as I have suggested, have two sources: our common experience of the world, and an inner experience of an extraordinary reality. Again, the following items are not meant to be an exhaustive list. This is merely a starting point for the serious student of Gnostic spirituality. As in Buddhism, Gnosticism starts from the ground up. That is, it starts where we find ourselves. If it seems dark and forboding, that is because it washes away all sentimentality and looks squarely into the face of existence itself. On this score, Gnosticism is very empirically based. Further on in the essentials, that grounding becomes somewhat looser by necessity. It is driven inside and deeper into the well of a hidden reality, which is expressed mythologically and abstractly. I do not spend time dealing with classic Gnostic myths. That is for others to do. This section is meant to lead up to that mytho-poetic moment of departure that each of us must experience for ourselves. The experience of myth beyond the scope of this work brings one closer to that reality that clothes truth in image, and serves as personal windows into the fullness of all spiritual reality. These points therefore, are not a stopping place, but a beginning point. It should be read as such.

## The Nine Points

### 1. Life is Tragic.

*A. Human Beings feel incomplete and lost,
and carry a deep longing within them.*

To say that life is difficult would be an understatement. The first Noble Truth of Buddhism is that life is suffering, caused through desire. I would say more precisely, life is tragic caused by the process of life itself. The material process of existence is survival of the organism, thus, the organism seeks to eat, avoid threat and danger, and to procreate. This is biological life. It is a process of desire, even when it is unconscious or instinct driven.

The idea that human beings are free is an oversimplification. This notion does not take into account the fact that life in the physical universe necessitates biological imperatives. That is, we are not free from the biological process that is life itself. The concept of Freedom is very limited when it comes to this process. One might even argue, as I will, that Human Beings are not even free from their own psychologically driven instincts - much like we are not free from our physical ones. This point is of significance within religious and philosophical understandings because it drives to the heart of the Human predicament. In most western traditions the problem of human existence is the predicament of being a free "creature" in a world where bad choices have enslaved us and created a material matrix that has "fallen" from some higher state of reality. These traditions say that humankind is sinful, and their sin is disobedience from the natural order of things which had a kind of primal perfection.

It seems strange to blame a physical process on beings trapped within that process, but that is exactly what most western traditions in religion and philosophy have done. So, consequently, humans are blamed for death, violence and injustice, when those problems exist within the physical process itself, and human consciousness simply becomes the quality that illuminated this flaw. To say that life is tragic is to simply state the human situation. We live in a world flawed with its own process - death, violence, injustice and a host of other observable and experiential issues that only humans with their ability to perceive consciously can attest to.

It is not a far stretch to understand why Human Beings would long for something more in a system like this. The question becomes: "Was this world of physical process "created" by some Divine mind, or did it just happen out of the cosmic deep?" Modern people increasingly have a difficult time believing that such a situation could have been designed by a loving deity. A "big bang" seems more plausible and likely, even though it, too, does not satisfy our thirst for meaning within this predicament. Many people just "check out" of thinking about this altogether. Kierkegaard called them "shut-up"—people who have become zombie-like in their living, with only the most superficial of understanding. They seek comfort and wish to avoid, at all costs, confrontation with the world that would make them think or feel the powerlessness of their existence. They flee into "faith" to avoid this confrontation, and take refuge in simplistic religions that keep them drugged with psychological magic to keep pain at bay. "Faith", in this sense, is the dark side of religion, because it requires blind obedience to a belief that runs contrary to experience and reason; a belief that faith itself will re-align the forces against them and turn tragedy into ease or at least meaningfulness. Unfortunately, life remains tragic, and our longing for "something more" continues unabated.

B.  *The physical world is blind process without moral regard.*
*We feel trapped and preyed upon.*
*Human beings struggle for meaning.*

It doesn't take long to figure out that the natural world does not care. That is a harsh reality to learn. Good people die. Bad people go on living, and sometimes quite well. There is no natural justice, even though we would like to think there is. Some may speculate about Karma, a kind of cause and effect justice to the universe, but because one's consciousness is erased by the reincarnation effect, justice is mitigated - not to mention the fact that many parts of the material world do not have a kind of mindfulness to them, and just are what they are. Viruses kill people not as some kind of divine justice, but rather because they are simply doing what viruses do - consume, just as human beings consume plant and animal life to simply live.

To make the statement that the physical world doesn't care, is actually a soft approach. Many could rightly say that the material world preys upon itself. In other words, it is predatory by nature. So the material world is at best indifferent to us, and at worst predatory toward us. The world is a kind of giant cafeteria. In a sense, life itself is merely a platform on which the struggle between beings and death occur. Death is the adversary, and even though we might say correctly that death is a natural part of life, something inside us recoils at the idea, and we do everything in our power to defeat its control over us.

Another troubling aspect of the physical world is its irrationality. It has no moral code, nor can it be reasoned with. To live is to feel a kind of power scramble, power in this sense used as the ability to control. To control one's environment becomes the first task. To find or build shelter from the elements and the dangers of physical life is an organizational principle of being human, indeed, of being alive in the world. Rain, tornadoes, hurricanes, earthquakes and the like never ask: "is this a good time for us to appear?" They are simply a product of a world that does not rationally ask questions of itself, but just acts. It does not care. Thus the world is a tragic trap.

2.   We recoil from the context of existence.

A.   *Human Beings become psychologically defended to protect themselves from the harshness of life.*

Because existence is cold, harsh and tragic, we begin to detach from our immediate experience of it. We construct patterns of thinking that serve as a barrier. These mental and emotional patterns are the subject of psychological study, which include the various forms of what has been termed defense mechanisms. These patterns, such as denial, rationalization, minimization and the like become unconscious to us. That is, they become automatic and through them we begin to construct an automatic focus. This defended state keeps us in an illusionary protection—a false sense of security about the world in which we live. It, in essence, keeps us from the terror of life that surrounds us all the time, and the utter vulnerability that we feel. It also hardens us to the inner alienation that is the truth of our existence, and obscures the spiritual light inside of us. This psychological magic is both a great power and a great enemy, for while it makes it possible to live day to day in the world of material process, it also covers over the more profound and deeper truth of ourselves. We begin to externalize ourselves, and attach our identity to the images we see of ourselves in the world. These images confirm our psychological defenses, and we begin to live a kind of shadow existence with only the shallowest sense of ourselves.

*B. Systems of law and order are generated to relieve our feelings of longing, injustice and alienation. We create a secondary reality of social, political, economic and religious patterns to distract ourselves from the terror and boredom of life.*

All social, political, economic and religious organization is a kind of secondary reality which keeps us defended in a physical and emotional way. Our psychological defenses materialize on the outside of us in the creation of these secondary realities. We strive to live apart from the blind process of the world even while we exist within it. We begin to absorb our sense of self into these organizational patterns, and they become our primary focus. These institutions take on a kind of life of their own through our focus on them, and they begin to consume all our time, effort and thinking. We lose ourselves all the more, and the intended distraction becomes a total loss of self in these secondary realities. These contrived patterns become our taskmasters, for which we conscript ourselves to die for, sacrifice for and zealously defend with great conviction and strength. Soon we are no longer aware that the institutions of our creation are only organized defenses against life itself. We empower them with "divine rights", and project transcendental reality to them, as an ironic metaphor for our own loss of self. We become unwitting slaves, unable to see our own enslavement.

*C. These secondary systems and patterns degenerate and begin to emulate the tragic material process they are meant to separate us from.*

Institutional systems require cognitive insight into their purposeful creation to keep them functioning as secondary reality forms to insulate us from the world. They begin to degenerate as we become absorbed into them and lose our sense of self. They begin to emulate the very process that we seek to avoid. People get forgotten and lost within them, and management of the systems becomes more concerned with survivability than compassion and security. They become secondary "food chains" in which the weaker individuals, those that cannot manipulate the system fast enough or good enough, get pushed into poverty, fear and homelessness. The more the system breaks away from its mindful purpose as a defense from the world, the more it fashions itself as a blind component of the world. In the 20th century, Nazi Germany became a kind of natural reality where unconscious force ruled with violence and terror. The secondary social and political reality merged with the natural material process and created ruthlessness and indiscriminate violence. Like lions chasing gazelle, the armies of the Third Reich rolled over the innocent as if evolution itself had become unrestrained. And that was precisely what happened - evolution had become unrestrained by the secondary systems, and the terror felt from living in the world became unmitigated.

To lesser degrees this degeneration occurs regularly, and the stress and strain of keeping our systems above the blind process of materiality becomes ever more difficult. We fear an apocalyptic end of the world as a religious event precisely because our secondary systems cannot be maintained and they bring us closer to the nature we dread. The possible collapse of these systems bring us to a marginal awareness of our terror of the natural world, and we think of these dissolutions as religious events, since they echo into the vacuum of our selflessness. Apocalyptic thinking, whether in Biblical texts or secular literature, is merely a projection of the fear that we cannot protect ourselves from the most basic dread of existence itself. Natural calamities such as earthquakes and the like, are given exaggerated importance and counted as judgment, because the psychic energy to keep our secondary systems of reality in place are fading. This makes it feel as if the world itself is coming apart.

The collapse of sociopolitical reality has been in progress from the very beginning of their creation. Even though it appears as if civilization and society have grown, particularly with the advent of technology, it in reality has been in the process of collapse for many generations. We simply don't have the psychic energy to create and sustain an artificial reality of this order, much like the creator god of Judeo-Christian myth who lacks the insight and ability to sustain his created order. The inevitability of tragedy is fixed into place.

### 3. Existence traps us into a circle of powerlessness

#### A. *No system, natural or artificial, alleviates the human condition.*

Society and civilization cannot save us, nor can our technology. They can make us comfortable for a time, but that comfort is only temporary and unstable at best. All our external efforts cannot tell us who we really are. In fact, they lead away from the deeper truth of our essential reality. The general tiredness felt among people today, as well as the rise in depression and anxiety, demonstrates the truth of our powerlessness.

People feel trapped, whether in dead end jobs, a bad relationship, poor health, or just the hustle and bustle of modern life. Fame or fortune, which we think will liberate us, just leads to greater loss of freedom. There is no way out, at least in the conventional sense. But this is just the outer shell of our entrapment. Deeper within there is always a sense of not fitting in, of not being entirely comfortable with our self in the world. Try as we may to escape, we get thrown back into the trap. All of our obsessions are attempted escapes that just lead to different traps. Nowhere is this more obvious than in the consumer culture of the modern world - where shopping becomes the attempt to fit in without loss of identity. The truth is that, within the natural process, loss is inevitable. More obvious still is the rigidity of the common orthodox religions that demand faith in a system, both social and biological, that will eventually dilute individuality to the point of being unrecognizable.

But the deeper trap is beneath all of its outward symbols - a kind of social consensual agreement we have with ourselves to maintain our sleep and intoxication with the world as a whole. We become as a consensual group, one dimensional thinkers. Even our so-called intellectuals cannot break out of their need to play the inner lie with themselves and others. They think of themselves as "free-thinkers", but their thought is not free at all, but a kind of agreed upon circle within a circle. Intellectualization and rigidity of common logic become unwitting partners in the entrapment of the human spirit. The packaging changes, but the items within remain the same. All the intellectual manipulation of words, as well as social and political systems become merely an animal pacing in a cage. The cage is the world that we are trying desperately to describe to ourselves, and yet, no thought is ever given to leaving the cage itself - for that seems unthinkable or impossible. The cage becomes everything. We design ways to cope - to harmonize ourselves with the cage in which we live. We think ourselves into becoming "one with" this or that, but that is merely becoming one with the cage itself. We try to convince ourselves to love our suffering and embrace it as if we are being given a lesson or a gift. But enslavement is never a gift or lesson - just torment. Which is why the alienation, powerlessness and entrapment never seems to leave us. We just feel it over and over again.

### B. Life feels empty and meaningless.

Small meanings permeate us and sustain us, because there is no larger meaning at all. We live for the small meanings in our lives - the love between us, or the satisfaction derived from some achieved inner goal. But these small meanings are never a replacement for the larger meaning that is not there. On occasion these small meanings fade away from our sight, and we view the emptiness. We get touched with the tragedy and pain of it all - like when a hero dies, or when something great gets lost.

Perhaps the greatest clue to our overwhelming aloneness and sense of meaninglessness is our obsession with UFOs, angels and miracles. All of these are designed to fill our emptiness, to project meaningful contact with an invisible world that, we hope, has an interest in our reality. We search the vastness of space for radio contact with aliens, and we watch the night skies to glimpse a look at something that will fill us with a momentary hope that we are not alone. Or, we sit and stare at the nightly television programs on such subjects as angels and the "unexplained" because inside of us we feel the distance between the vastness of existence and the "I" that witnesses it all.

Beyond the wonder of looking at the high heavens, with all its points of light, is a kind of longing. A longing built with a sense of having been abandoned here - for what reason and how, we cannot quite touch with all our intellect. This inner sense of abandonment is affected by the meaninglessness that surrounds us daily. We strive to *know* in a world that blocks our knowing.

47

Why else would creatures in this world feel as if they have no belonging here unless, in some strange way, they are not altogether from this reality.

### 4. We are aliens

#### A.  *The truth of our predicament pushes us to sense an otherness inside ourselves.*

Our sense of abandonment, aloneness and meaninglessness becomes the greatest insight into who we really are.  In a real sense, all of our visions of UFO's, angels, miracles and aliens are simply projections of who we are.  We come to acknowledge that we are "other than" this world of material process, even while so obviously a part of it.

Throughout history, but even more so now than ever before, reports of abductions by alien forces or beings permeates our popular culture.  Before the popularity of extraterrestrial abduction, there was abduction by werewolves or vampires or the various population of figures that are recounted in folklore and myth.  We have never felt quite safe; not quite bound to the earth the way that we have reasoned we should.  At the deepest levels, we feel that something strange could over take us suddenly, and in a moment of time we could disappear into some region beyond this world.  We fear this abduction, but long for it .  It is as strange and threatening, as it is inviting and welcoming.  But in the final analysis it is our own alien nature that is at work.

All the strangeness that is felt, although terrifying, is also illuminating.  The emptiness and even the predatory character of the world in which humans find themselves, also leads the individual, if aware, to a sense of being more than the world that encases them. While the experience of the world is vacant of meaning, the interior world is filled with the questions of meaning and a multitude of images that reference something deeper within that cannot be easily expressed. The development of myth points to the essence of this other reality that is felt in and through the experience of emptiness.

Every tale of a hero traversing dangerous and frightening worlds is our own tale being told to us by this other inner reality. Like the hero of these myths, we are alone and are in need of courageous conviction and knowledge to be able to make the difficult journey into the world of our true home. We are the lost prince or princess, finding allies and enemies along the way. We find ourselves put to sleep by something evil and vile, then awakened by something pure and beautiful so the journey can continue. This is the stuff of myth, and also the stuff of our awakening to who we really are. The inner world pushes us to something more.

> B.  *This otherness is a window into a higher reality
> beyond all matter and energy, which is an alien
> presence identified as the "spirit" or "spark".*

The stories told within ourselves suggest a higher reality to which we ultimately belong. They are as a finger pointing the way. This reality is unlike the empty world of material existence, but rather full and rich - beyond description and illustration. It is referenced through our inner experience, and yet is beyond that experience in a mysterious kind of way.

Our alienation from the concrete ordinary world of existence guides us to the extraordinary - a simple window into  the truth that we are more than we had thought of ourselves. Our awakened spirit begins to grow.

## 5. We begin to unfold.

### *A. We awaken to the spirit trapped within a hardened reality that is rigidly focused upon the world of physicality, emotionality, and mental process.*

As we begin the awakening process, great realizations occur. We experience ourselves being too narrowly focused, and we begin to observe ourselves differently than before. We observe ourselves being lost amidst concerns and worries, frustrations and desires. We begin to see that those things that had been our alienated life in the small reality of the world, were also forces within ourselves - like tiny blinders that kept us from seeing larger truth.

Not only is the material world a place of emptiness, but that emptiness itself is part of our makeup as well. It is a kind of small self from which we must relieve ourselves. The drives of the objective world become apparent - the biological imperatives and the forces within us that are natural to that world. We also become aware that those secondary systems of social and political order are no less driven and enslave our spirit within the tight circles of narrowly focused realities. We are forced to rethink ourselves, and place our automatic beliefs, behaviors and emotions within a more mindful context. This is a confusing time for those awakening. Nothing seems solid, since old ideas, understandings and ways of living are beginning to fade into a deeper truth. Within this confusion we re-visit our lostness again and again, as we have need of its truth to keep us away from the old patterns and habits. Our vision of the world becomes blurred, no longer a simple small focus upon survival and mundane emotional happiness.

## *B. We are pulled toward the inner reality, and loosened from our fixed point of focus.*

The knowledge (gnosis) of this separate and higher reality begins to "call" to us, like some sweet siren of myth. Our dissatisfaction with the ordinary world is complete. Our alienation validated, and the truth of our inner identity begins to unfold - like the lotus flower of Buddhist symbolism. This unfolding loosens us from our fixed small reality, and our thirst for the "other" reality becomes powerful. Our outlook changes. To those on the outside of this experience, it appears as if the person is someone completely different, identified within by a different definition.

The attention of the awakened becomes energetically intended toward liberation. The boundaries of common thought, social convention and ordinary concern are loosened as well. To be awake is to think differently about oneself and the world, and to walk with deliberation toward the higher reality that sets one free from all contrivances. The world is no less heavy with tragedy and suffering, and yet, the awakened spirit knows that its reality is but short —its power illusory.

This time of awakened unfolding is a time of soul-consciousness. We must see the relationship between one's self in the world and one's larger self outside of the world. The journey becomes two-fold: passing through the world, and detaching from it. Both aspects occur simultaneously. Soul consciousness looks with compassion at a sea of spirit engulfed by hardening matter; weighing it down into muck and mire. The unfolding, awakening, soul-conscious individual cares to listen and love even those that are so lost within the darkness that they cannot see who they truly are. Knowledge of the true self begins to make itself visible everywhere, and in the world of darkness and despair - the mysterious spirit illuminates everything in its true nature. Life becomes liberated beyond the context of the mundane and ordinary, and the magic of the spirit revealed becomes more clear in every moment.

### 6. Our Spiritual True Self has been revealed through various individuals throughout human history.

*A. Many great teachers have become so identified with the spirit that they have served as observable windows into this "other" reality.*

To sit with the inner reality as it grows in strength is to begin to identify with it. The Buddha sat under the Bodhi tree (tree of knowledge) until he was awake. In that awakened spirit he was the other reality itself being presented in spoken and tender ways to people lost within the weight of the world. To become awakened like Siddhartha many centuries ago, or the many others who, in their way, became awakened and alive with its truth, is to be filled with the gnosis. But it is much more than that. It allows the dissolution of the small self which drives our daily lives with all its petty concerns and worries, and brings forth into our physical being a transcendental spirit that literally merges with us and becomes us. No longer, then, are we who we were.

That is what occurred with the great teachers of gnosis. A spiritual reality literally spoke through them from that other world. That is the nature of revelation itself. It reveals itself from some other world, whose intent is to instruct the hearer toward the light of that other reality. More than simply identifying with the myths about such a otherworldly reality, they become that reality. Many such people have lived among us.

*B. Through these "windows" the gnosis of a completely separate reality is confirmed.*

The work of most great teachers has been to confirm and illuminate the reality of the other world. That was their primary mission. That is, their focus toward us was and remains instructional and conformational. Their work, in that way, is foundational to anything else, and in no way subordinates them to any other great teacher of the gnosis. All great teachers have had their focus and mission. To make a list of these teachers would be impossible, for not all are publicly known. Also, not all that are assumed to be great teachers, are. Remember, the great teachers of gnosis instruct about the other reality, and only marginally, and as a side effect, give laws and rules for living here in this world - for this world becomes more transparent to the Gnostic who has now seen something more.

The great Gnostic teachers that many religious traditions celebrate, spoke on different levels and with different intent, depending on the hearer. The teachings of these great ones, therefore, are understood differently by those who are awake to the gnosis they carry, and more concrete to those that are not aware. We see only what we can see. The stories and parables of these teachers act at the levels that people can access them, and in themselves can become agents of awakening. The more one reads them, the more one may see.

Unfortunately, most religious traditions have centered around surface understandings of their own teachings, and thereby blocked the gnosis they are meant to deliver. This is why most religions leave people with a sense of emptiness and longing for more. Those who see this truth, may remain in a religious tradition, but see more within it than is generally acceptable, and usually find themselves in conflict with the religious authorities.

Respect for these great teachers is important, and no one teacher is greater than another - their work is just different. The divisions created in this area represent the chaos inherent in the world - which has a natural drive to separate things.

7. The decisive revelation of this separate reality was presented
   in Jesus of Nazareth, who is called "The Christ."

*A. Although Jesus is not the only revealer of this other reality,*
*he remains the clearest presentation of it.*

The "Christ" descended upon Jesus of Nazareth for a
specific work, namely the liberation of the spirit from the bondage
of the world. The Christ, as an aspect of the divine reality, came
upon the man named Jesus and literally spoke through him. The
Christ, therefore, can be said to be separate from, yet revealing
itself through the person of Jesus. The Christ was not physical
nor could it die; it was not subject to the laws of this world, and
spoke clearly the words of liberation that awakens the inner light
to its true origin. To say that The Christ died upon the cross for
the sins of humankind is an error, for The Christ was and is a
spiritual quality beyond the realm of death and corruptibility.

As The Christ walked in the person of Jesus of Nazareth,
a clear and decisive presentation of the other reality was revealed.
He taught the path that leads from darkness of the world into the
true light of the divine essence.

*B. The Christ's mission was to reveal the spiritual truth of*
*who we are, and be a guide to this separate reality from*
*which we have come.*

Both privately and publicly The Christ, through Jesus,
gave instruction as to the reality of our true nature, and sought to
release the spirit from its bondage in the physical world of
darkness. His teachings are both direct and hidden within
parables and sayings that are meant to knock on the door of the
soul to awaken the spirit within. The work and goal of The Christ
was to loosen the attachment of the spirit from the thickness of the
lower material realm. Every teaching must be read in this way for

them to reveal the world to which The Christ spoke. Apocalyptic and moralistic sayings attributed to Jesus are additions by the orthodox church to control and frighten people into greater subservience, and all references of the Kingdom coming upon this world are further attempts to keep the spirit enslaved to the world by unawakened individuals who are lost within a narrow and hurtful mindset.

The decisive clarity of the other reality is revealed in the teachings of The Christ, and in no way are represented in the manner of death that Jesus incurred upon the cross. The cross is more accurately a symbol of the tragic context of the world in which humans find themselves. As The Christ came upon Jesus of Nazareth, his life fundamentally altered and revealed a life unattached from the restraints and restrictions of ordinary convention. He thus "prepared a way" for people to walk through life becoming themselves liberators. To accept the truth of one's true self is to be free. To see the work of The Christ is to see the work of a liberator-moving in the thickness of the world and stating clearly that he is not "of the world," even as we are not.

## 8. We become the greater reality now.

### A. Understanding this revealed knowledge awakens us to our true origin, and brings about an authentic change of awareness.

Gnosis changes our lives. Our awareness of the world and of the spirit intensifies, and our life in the world becomes a warrior's journey through a strange land. Our ego is loosened, and our fixation on the material world is lessened. We begin to see that all the contrivances of social organization are only shadows - that our true home is elsewhere, beyond the scope of anything this universe can hold. We are awakened to a new sense of self - larger and fuller than anything we might have imagined in a previous time, and yet, this new self needs far less from anyone and anything. Mundane concerns begin to fade. Ordinary family matters feel less straining, as do all other matters of this world - for we have realized that they have nothing to do with who we really are, and have nothing to do with getting us back to the world from which we have come. Our reality becomes our sense of knowing who we are. All laws and actions are subjugated to this knowledge, for they are products of this world and everything about this world is a constraint upon the spirit. Truly, the Gnostic assumes complete and total responsibility for everything in this existence, since what we do or think is relevant and judged only in terms of our inner light. This never means that the Gnostic freely commits acts of crime or injustice, quite the contrary. The Gnostic lives by higher standards, knowing that all laws and rules are corrupted.

Acquiring gnosis enables one to see behind the imagines and forms to the deeper truth. To be a Gnostic is to see the chains fall away, and to be awake to those who have also come into the light of their true self. The Gnostic becomes a Christ to others - offering a sense of freedom in a world of bondage. Not worried about what the world thinks or does, the Gnostic liberates through becoming, as The Gospel of Thomas puts it, "passersby" (vs. 42). Also, the gnosis draws us together. Those who are awake seek one another, for to stay awake becomes the important point of living. The Gnostic community becomes the community of the awakened - the true human being. Although the Gnostic may decide to separate himself/herself from the world of the ordinary, there is always a longing for the light that resides within to be awakened in all people. The sense of the tragic world does not go away, but it is give a new context from which to be understood. Joy becomes the hallmark of the Gnostic journey, for the Gnostic knows where home is, and even while in the world, knows the fullness awaits.

## B. *Through gnosis human beings are freed from fear.*

I have heard it said that fear is "false evidence appearing real." Fear of the world is always false evidence appearing real. Once awakened the spirit has power over all false powers and forces. That does not mean that the spirit can change the course of a river or change the blind process of the world. It means that the spirit has escaped the forces that seek to keep it trapped in darkness. This is no small release, for to be liberated from the fear of continual enslavement makes one strong and alive to the freedom that is forthcoming in every movement toward the world of the spirit. Fear binds one to something - an attachment that holds someone in place like an emotional glue. When our lives lack gnosis, the fear of life captivates and surrounds us. Everything becomes about creating security and safety, not liberation and authentic freedom. The gnosis frees us first from fear, for in the world of true spirit, fear is not a reality - for it knows beyond all else that nothing can ultimately separate it from its divine source. Fear is an emotional attachment to the world of materiality. The Gnostic awakens to the reality that the worst has already occurred. That is, that the spirit has fallen into the world of falsehood and darkness, and now, through its awakening, begins the journey home. Thus, what is there to fear? Homecoming is near. The power of the darkness is broken, and once broken, the first steps toward the world of the spirit begins. Joy becomes the hallmark of the Gnostic's life - for every step is a step toward home. Yes, each step is filled with peril, and yet the peril is nothing compared with the danger of having slept to the truth of self. So even the peril is accepted with joy, for the perilous journey lasts only for a little while - an illusion of time, and then, it is over. That is the Gnostic's gift, this knowledge that enables inner peace within a world of suffering and death.

## 9. To remain asleep is to remain in the tragic context of the world.

*A.   Those who remain unawakened to this separate reality continue to be stuck in the world, and revisit over and over their lostness and terror.*

There are consequences to the unawakened life - the tragedy of the world continues unabated. The feelings of being forlorn and lost, alienated and fearful drive one deeper and deeper into the material context. Like monkeys swinging through trees fleeing danger, the unawakened move back and forth in their life without knowing what drives them or why they feel the way they do. Comfort or anger become their guiding principles, because both are driven by hopelessness and fear.

This continual return into the darkness is multi-leveled which has physical, emotional and spiritual aspects to it. Like gravity, the pressure and force of the world moves the unawakened person to activities, thoughts and instincts that are all subject to the material matrix. Carl Jung spoke of this as being a complex that one unconsciously activates and literally lives within, both in terms of behavior and thought patterns. But there is also a deeper and more metaphysical dimension to this continual return. The spark or the spirit that is enslaved to the material world literally continues to stay caught, and enacts the nature of that entrapment over and over again until awakening occurs. This blind process of continual return is the essence of material reality, and functions like a loop in which the cycle is repeatedly played out. This continual return loop has no orientation toward spiritual instruction, nor is it a system of natural justice. It is simply and merely blind process that slings the unawakened spirit back into the world placing it into the random nature of material reality.

The awakened spirit escapes this cycle through gnosis itself. That is a simple knowing of the difference between itself and the process it finds itself in. Aware of its true nature, the spirit witnesses the passageway between the worlds and simply wills itself into the separate reality of the fullness, where it is helped and loved into its true reality.

The nature and fundamental characteristics of the "Pleroma" or "Fullness" cannot be explained or spoken of through language. Like the spirit itself, it cannot be said to exist in any way in which we understand existence other than the utter total love and freedom that resides within. The Gnostic knows that the True Self belongs to this separate reality - this other world. In this knowledge, the Gnostic derives strength, purpose and knowledge.

*B. Since the Spirit is totally alien to the world of energy and matter, ultimately upon the death of the universe all spiritual quality will be released from its bondage.*

Valentinus, the great Gnostic theologian of the second century, once wrote that Gnostics are to "make death die". He wrote that to be awake and aware was to literally begin the process of making death itself die - that is, to hasten the death of the universe through simply denying it the life essence it derives from the spirit. From the Gnostic point of view, the universe is already a "corpse" (Gospel of Thomas vs. 56). It is destined to die since it cannot sustain itself beyond the scope of its own nature - which is self-consumption. The liberation longed for by the awakened spirit, therefore, is already upon it, even as the spirit moves through the material world. The worst that can happen to the spirit has already happened. The falling of the Spirit into this world of darkness. But, the darkness is being dissolved, and each Gnostic participates in the dying of death through their own gnosis. The Christ is said to have laughed at death as it fled the cross, and as each Gnostic sees the truth, that same laughter rings out upon the world in ever increasing volume.

One might see this like a snowball that has encapsulated a pebble. As the snow melts the pebble is freed from its icy cage. This is, in a sense, what is happening with the world. It melts away, revealing the hidden treasure it has trapped within. Ultimately, the Gnostic hope is based upon the passing away of the false dark reality, both through the efforts of the Gnostics themselves, and the deficiency of material reality. When energy and matter are no more, the "Alien Within" is free and the fullness of Pleroma remains as it has always been - the many within the one - the true divine whole.

## Some Follow Up Notes

These essential points of Gnosticism are small steps into the larger world of Gnostic thinking. The realization that there is something more going on than simply the process of existence, is in this understanding, the first moment of spiritual awakening. Not all Gnostics agree as to how gnosis is understood and conceptualized. Gnostics tend toward radically individual approaches, which have been their downfall in terms of creating and sustaining church organizations. The most basic Gnostic doctrine, if it can be called that, is simply the questions of who we are, why we are here and where we are going. How did this world of suffering and tragedy come to be, and how might I traverse it with the greatest of ease and joy, and not fall prey to its traps? These are the cornerstones of Gnostic thinking. When the Gnostic looks out upon the world, he/she does not just see vast wonder. The Gnostic, more importantly, sees the questions that the vastness presents - with all the conscious sense of what it feels like to find oneself in the midst of all of it.

Gnosticism has a kind of basic honesty about life and our inner world - our fears and our longings. That Gnosticism would be called "Christian heresy" speaks volumes on the deficiency of the orthodox approach. The terror of the material system that humans find themselves in plagues their religions, too. Christianity became what it initially began to expose - the murderous, controlling and intoxicating world. Perhaps that is why the orthodox church fathers were endlessly accusing the Gnostics of one foul deed after another - those same deeds were buried within them and were only being projected upon those whom they feared.

It has taken us a great while to see the actual terror committed by the orthodox church in the name of the Creator God. Perhaps they were acting as they should, being worshipers of a deity whose very actions and utterances are dipped in blood. When they eliminated the Gnostics from their ranks, they eliminated the only real challenge to their control and power ; those who claimed inner knowledge as their guide, not church authority or totalitarian rule by Bishops and Popes. Yes, indeed, the issues were theological, as well as political. Yes, it became personal and horrifying.

Those who buried the Gnostic Scriptures at Nag Hammadi, Egypt, were probably very well aware of how much those documents meant, and at what risk they were in to simply have them. They saved them for a more enlightened time, or at least a time when the power of the orthodox rulers would wane. They are not ordinary gospels in the sense we now think of gospels. They are not meant to be history, nor tell the life story of an individual, but rather to speak in mytho-poetic language about a separate reality beyond the scope of any factual account of historical events. They tell of our true origin, beyond birth and death, to another world of image and abstraction which seems strange and peculiar, since we have been trained not to think in these terms. But, they are alive with something that resonates within us – something that is alien to this world.

## Truth, Myth and Aquaintance

While those within orthodox religion argue about the historical fact of special births, or of miracles outside of the natural order, and the meaning of history itself, the Gnostics are much more concerned with inner revelation and becoming aware of something higher inside of themselves. History, like nature itself, is just a process - not saving, as many orthodox theologians would insist. It does not reveal truth, nor lend itself easily as a window to something more inside us as people. In fact, history is but the process of our secondary systems being pushed along by our psychological needs. Events and institutions in history tend to do more to distract than they do to illuminate.

It is because of this that Gnostics were not interested in recounting historical events around the life of any religious figure. They were interested in the teachings, and in the mythic imagery ; not factual events. No event has meaning outside of the inner world that perceives it. The events of history are not truth, and the early Gnostics knew well this reality. History reveals merely our philosophical bankruptcy and delusion, a kind of negative truth, if you will. And yet, within all this is an inner dynamic that projects itself onto the hardened landscape of material reality. The Gnostics, among others, were interested in this truth inside, not its shadow as it appears in the world. Thus, Gnostic scriptures are populated with imaginative images, and figures appearing in a world beyond. Readers are invited into a dream - a kind of separate reality where perception is turned on its head - and the beginning is of greater importance than the end. This is the way to truth - that each would discover their beginning, not their end; that one would look inside for reality, not to the outside. Strangely, the Gnostics were in ancient times, psychologically modern.

This inner world of reality beyond the scope of materiality has a kind of consciousness to it - where it, in its own way, has life and inner mindfulness. And yet, having said this, it must be immediately stated that this inner world of dream and imagination, where myth is born and reborn, is not the alien world itself. It is merely a bridge to a realm beyond itself. Perhaps it is best said that this inner world is the soul connection with the spirit. It is the interconnection between the two worlds - where the alien spirit, meets the energy world of the soul, which in turn meets the material world. The spirit cannot be experienced like one might experience something in the world. The meaning of the word "gnosis" is really acquaintance, for that is what finally occurs. Gnosis is not an experience of the spirit, but rather an acknowledgment of the spirit becoming acquainted with itself and its own world. This acknowledgment we often take as experience, as it feels that way to us in a fashion. And yet, it is so much more.

The core of Gnosticism is basically an acquaintance with the spirit. Awakening is a movement: becoming aware of self in the material world, moving to seeing oneself psychologically, to experiencing the deep well of myth, and finally the alien spirit knowing itself. If we can speak of evolving consciousness, it is only in this inner manner that it makes sense. This process of inner evolution moves back and forth as we journey through life, seeing repeatedly the doorway between the realities.

## Gnosticism Today

*"Whoever finds himself is superior to the world"*...

-The Gospel of Thomas

To identify oneself as a Gnostic is to say that one has become aware of the awakening of the spirit to its own alien world. There are no religious doctrines involved, save that of knowing the separate reality of Spirit. There are no set rituals, although many rituals may be helpful in leading to the mystery that is Spirit. Gnosticism is a perspective, not a religion. Thus, the Gnostic cannot be pigeon-holed and placed into a single box. No body of literature can contain Gnosticism, nor can any single definition be full enough to describe who a Gnostic is. Gnostics may meet, discuss and maybe even create and sustain a church, but never will the church become more than the gnosis that brought the people together. The true church is an inner reality of being, not a visible presentation, or even an invisible collective concept, and certainly not a political organization of Clergy, Bishops and Popes. To be a Gnostic is to be, as Jesus put it, "in the world but not of it"; to be "a passerby", and as such the Gnostic finds no true home here in this world.

For many, Gnosticism will be strange and disturbing, a challenge to everything that has been taught and believed. It will alarm their sensitivities, and insult their lifestyle. It will scare those who wish to make more of this world than it is, for it will intensely confront the idea that there is any real meaning in this dark place other than in recognizing its shadow nature. Gnosticism will rock the world of conventional religion, since the authority of their books and professional staff is but an aspect of false comfort. Orthodoxy lulls people to sleep with ignorance, violence and sheer stupidity. It will seem destabilizing to those who comply with the status quo, and appear detached and uncommitted to the "good hearted" liberal.

But to those who have touched their alienation and awkwardness in the world, Gnosticism will be a fresh wind. To those who can see no hope here, and have given up, and to those who feel forced into the rigidity of religious and political forms that they cannot tolerate, Gnosticism will be a liberation. For those who are uncomfortable and have found no way to make sense of the world, Gnosticism will speak truth.

> What makes us free is the Gnosis
> of who we were
> of what we have become
> of where we were
> of wherein we have been thrown
> of whereto we are hastening
> of what we are being freed
> of what birth really is
> of what rebirth really is

This Gnostic credo from the second century speaks loudly and clearly today. Truly, there could not be a time and a people more in need of Gnostic truth. We feel that we have been thrown into a world of tragedy. We are pulled along without pause to reflect—enslaved to a shadow from which we must be freed. No religion or institution bound to the earth can free the spirit, only that which comes from the spirit itself - the gnosis - can achieve that great end. For when we make the end like the beginning, shall our liberation be upon us, and the alien spirit will return to its place of origin—the True Home.

## Appendix A – Atonement Theology

*"...they threw mankind into great distraction and into a life of toil, so that their mankind might be occupied by worldly affairs, and might not have the opportunity of being devoted to the holy spirit."*

-The Hypothesis of the Archons

"In the beginning when God created the Heavens and the Earth...it was good." In the dominant religious belief of Judaism and Christianity, creation has a quality of goodness to it. Not just that it is beautiful and grand, but it is good - a moral quality of being in line with the creator's wishes and will. The harmony of nature, in those first creative moments, which perhaps can be seen as billions of years, were morally good. That is to say, they were within the will of the creator, who understood Himself to be good, therefore it was good as it issued forth from His will and His intention. The early texts do not say that the created order was loving, although it is implied in its "goodness". God loved it. He was satisfied with it, and so He rested, the text says.

On this, all of dominant Christian theology hangs. The belief that the world was created in goodness and love is followed by the idea that humankind was created free - with a will from which to act and behave. Thus, the story goes, humankind was placed down into the garden, and there through free will, chose to disobey God's orders not to eat from the forbidden Tree of Knowledge. The "Original Sin" occurred, where upon the entire created order was plunged into darkness. Death came upon the world through the sin of Adam and Eve, the Old Testament claims, which forced humankind to suffer and die - not because the world was deficient, but because they had disobeyed God and become "sinners".

The next theological steps take us to God's anger. He was angry that He, the Lord God, had been disobeyed. He cast Adam and Eve out of the garden into a harsh and cruel existence. They were forced into a life of hardship and pain because of their disobedient behavior. Because of their separation from God, humankind was forced to make sacrifices to please this angry and hostile power. God was pleased by the sacrifices of Abel, who supplied God with the best he had, while Cain, who kept back some of the best for himself, was displeasing in God's sight. Cain killed Abel, because God favored him, and God's anger swelled even more. Eventually, the story goes, God was so angry that He decided to wash human beings out of his sight, except a small band led by a man named Noah. This God did out of his wrath. Afterwards God was sad, and said that he would never do this kind of indiscriminate murder again, and pledged himself to this and sealed it with the mark of the rainbow.

In time, God sought to reconcile Himself to humankind again. He elected a people to deliver the message of his truth, and set before them His law. But again, as the dominant Christian Church would tell it, the law was inadequate to bring about this reconciliation, since humankind was so lost amidst sin. Even the prophets themselves were ignored and killed, as Cain had killed Abel, and God's wrath grew again. But God's love for the original goodness of the world would not let Him destroy humankind, and so God sent His only son into the world to die on the cross for the sins of humanity, and forever reconciling whosoever believed in him back into the original goodness from which the world had come. In time, God was to once again bring about the perfect world for this newly reconciled humankind to enjoy. That was the hope of the faithful.

Within what is now called "Atonement Theology" - the dominant theology of the Christian Church, the system looks like this:

1. God created a perfect world with the innate moral quality of goodness. It was completely within His will, and the harmony of nature was an expression of his truth.

2. God created human beings, who through an act of rebellion against God "fell" into sin and death, which contaminated the created world - since humankind had been given dominion over it - and henceforth death and violence came into the created order blocking the basic goodness of the world. This was the "Original Sin'.

3. Human beings became alienated from God and each other,

and their sin was passed down through the generations as the most fundamental of sexually transmitted diseases.

4.  God was angry.

5.  In time God sought to reconcile himself to humankind though the giving of the law, and he gave this law to an elect group of people for its keeping and safe guarding.

6.  The law, in and of itself proved to be insufficient, so God sent His "only begotten Son" to perform an act of sacrifice to atone for the sins of humankind. He became the fulfillment of the intention of the law. Because humankind was tainted with "original sin", it was necessary that Jesus have a specialized birth not marked by the sinfulness of humanity.

7.  Believing in Jesus as the true path to God, sinners are able to be reconciled to God in which God turns away from His anger, and remembers sin no more. Jesus becomes the "new Adam" where upon all believers are forgiven of their "original sin" and placed within the context of the family of God. "Original Sin" is not destroyed, but overcome through the redemptive act of Jesus.

8.  The created world is to be reconciled to God through a cleansing end time restoration of the perfect world through a dramatic confrontation between the forces of good and evil. "Original Sin" will be destroyed and the entire created order will be released from its bondage.

9.  The reconciled human community will again live at peace with the perfect world where Jesus himself will rule as the divine Son of God.

This, with variations, is the dominant belief espoused by the orthodox systems - which include all branches of Protestantism, as well as Catholicism. The foundation of this system is the idea that the "creation" had/has a quality of "goodness" to it, and that the reason for suffering and pain is human error and sin. Human Beings are to be good stewards of this good world, which we have not been, and therefore the resultant alienation.

However, as the scientific era blossomed in the 19th and 20th centuries, it became apparent that death was here before human beings set foot upon the earth. Fossils of dinosaurs abound, evidence that they are millions of years older than any human remains. Death was part of the system long before humankind committed any act, let alone a sinful one. In point of fact, to ascribe any moral quality to the physical world aside from the consciousness of human beings seems rather strange. The material universe looks more like a giant cafeteria than anything else. Those creatures that do not run fast enough, or are not smart enough get eaten. Some have literally been eaten for all time. They are gone. The universe of material being is basically a predatory one, where life is worked out in a genetic rush towards traits that enable a species to survive. To blame human beings for the harshness of this system, who by scientific accounts are the best predators to date - save that of certain viruses that will in the end, no doubt, be humankind's undoing, is simply putting the cart before the horse.

Perhaps the world is not a good place. Perhaps it never was, nor ever will be. It is a predatory cafeteria, that fuels its engine by feeding upon itself. Like Ouroborous, the snake of antiquity that was shown consuming its own tail. The world feeds on its own excrement, and fertilizes itself with the blood and bone of every creature that ever inhabited physicality.

To say, as most western religious forms have, that the world was created in goodness, seems to be a gross overstatement of its quality. The world itself is death incarnate. It gives and then takes away. It does not reason, nor hear the cry of those in pain. It rolls. It moves. It eats. That is its way. Yet, it is beautiful and grand. It is in many ways glorious and awesome. But we cannot

confuse beauty with goodness and love, as so many do in their
relationships. Radical environmentalists who worship the earth
and blame human beings for the harshness of life, simply miss the
point. Human beings have no real dominion over the earth. We,
of course, wish we did. It scares us. It overwhelms us. It terrifies
us. We seek in almost everything we do to protect ourselves from
it. We seek shelter from the elements. We seek refuse from its
cold impersonal process through the warmth of our mate, and the
meaning of our symbols and rituals. True enough, as some would
point out, we make matters worse when we foul the air and
contaminate the water. We destroy ourselves. We live longer and
better than ever before, but even as our attempts to keep ourselves
alive and safe from the harshness of the physical world confound
the system more, we cannot escape the reality of our fragility and
alienation from it. Our future, as some have pointed out, looks
bleak. Global warming and the destruction of the ozone are
enemies of our survival. So are the tiny viruses and germs that
make their home inside of us and threaten our lives. We are all
too aware of our limitations. If global warming doesn't get us,
something will, if not collectively, then individually. We each feed
the system. It is, on some fundamental levels, impossible to
protect ourselves from the cycle of life and death, which requires
our surrender to the cycle itself.

Some have wondered whether human beings have a kind of
death wish, so angry at life and the alienation that cannot be
alleviated, that we unconsciously, if not consciously, do things that
destroy ourselves. Human Beings seem trapped between two
opposing desires: one to live, and one to just "have it end". Viktor
Frankl in his timeless book Man's Search for Meaning describes
concentration camp prisoners who had tired of the horror of the
camps. He said that others always knew when someone had given
up. Everyone knew they would be dead shortly. We see this
same phenomenon among our inner city children who, growing
up amidst great poverty and violence, decide to join the ranks of
those who give up and just wait to be executed - either by the
system, or by their own companions. We see it among the host of

people who have dissolved themselves in front of the television set or computer screen, seeking as it were to disappear into another reality.

We blame ourselves. All of the dominant theological and political notions about the world turn the blame on human beings. If we were just better somehow, if we could just get in synch with the "Will of God" for our lives, or if we weren't such stupid sinners and got our act together, the world would be a better place. Compassion runs thin when we talk about ourselves, particularly when it comes to the kind of rugged individualistic philosophy that is so often religiously subscribed to. "Pull yourself up by your boot straps", the common theme where work makes everything right - good Judeo-Christian work ethics. But work doesn't make everything right. In fact, work has become less and less meaningful for more and more people. There is no pay-off. Even those who have so much have discovered, as spiritual leaders have always taught, that comfort is just the soft underside of terror.

The world terrorizes and overwhelms us. Its raw concreteness and cold process leave us in a state of perpetual shock. We are born, as ancient mystics observed, between feces and urine with tears in our eyes - crying from the moment we draw breath. Our alienation slaps us hard, even as we begin to feel our own sense of self that ignites panic and fear when we are still quite young. Inside of us is a consciousness that dreams and whose reality is fluid and deep, and yet we are bound and trapped in a body filled with the fragility of physical biology. This conflict never goes away. We are gods that shit. We are stuck.

Is the world good, and we are free to make of it whatever we want? Or, is it that the world is not all that good, and we are not all that free? Who, or what is to blame for our sad state of affairs? Has it been better in the past? Will it get better in the future? Is there any hope at all? These are the questions that we ask today, whether we explicitly realize it or not. Those ancient questions still live within us: Who am I? Why am I here? Where am I going? The answers of the dominant churches and the dominant political forms shaped by them, have given us little but self-recrimination and blame. Theology and politics have been more about power and control, than about truth. Perhaps the greater truth is that we, as human beings, are much more victims than perpetrators. We certainly tend to do to ourselves what the harsh material system of the world does to us. We become what brutalizes us. Like a highly born kidnapped victim - we begin to identify with our captors. The highest part of us creates systems that care for those who cannot care for themselves. The lowest part of us begins to emulate the predatory material system of the world. We call it honestly enough "Social Darwinism". Perhaps we practice this social Darwinism as a way to punish ourselves for the blame we affix to our "nature". As the blame and shame we have heaped upon ourselves lures us into a kind of walking unconsciousness concerning the reality of the world, our socioeconomic systems begin to look exactly like that which we want to escape - a food chain. We start consuming ourselves.

It is little wonder, given the gap between religious belief and scientific examination, that many find themselves in a religious vacuum. Many search within the context of "New Age" quasi-religions that seek to help people feel better about being here. But in the final analysis they fall prey to the same error as does the traditional orthodox religions that they seek to escape. They lack a kind of deep existential look at the world, just as the "feel good" churches of Protestant evangelicalism do. Positive thinking theology is just code for denial - the "don't ask" syndrome.

But amidst the religious vacuum created by the tension between the dominant theological systems and existential analysis is a kind of longing for a deeper truth that draws the passion of religious awakening into the reality of existential understanding. As the Gnostic Gospels of early Christianity, discovered at Nag Hammadi in 1946, have become translated and more widely distributed and read - something of a new awakening is occurring.

This awakening which is being felt in many Christian Churches is the realization that the dominant system of Christianity is not the only system of Christianity, and like the church of old, the battle for "the truth" of Christianity is beginning again.

Gnosticism takes the same ideas and teaching of Christ, and turns them on end. They are more psychologically oriented, and have a rich and full mythology that are at once unfamiliar and exciting, but have a kind of modernity to them. They make us think!

## Appendix B – The Real World

*"...ignorance ...brought about anguish and terror. And
the anguish grew solid like a fog, so that no one was
able to see. For this reason error is powerful..."*

-The Gospel of Truth

If the first statement of atonement theology is incorrect - that the world was created good, then the entire system begins to fall. One has to ask, if the world was not created good, then in what way or manner was it created at all? Was it created mindfully, and therefore with some evil or malicious intent? Or, is it just mindless process seeking itself, without intent or any particular malevolence? Or perhaps it was created mindfully, and without malicious intent, but just inadequate and without the kind of fullness needed to make the creation loving and kind. And then there is the issue of our judging something as big as the universe. Who are we that we would judge it to be deficient? God asks Job such a question, but then again, we know because we have read the prologue in the Book of Job, that all the suffering Job is visited with is but a result of a wager between God and Satan - which Job does not deserve, by God's own admission when he states Job's blamelessness. Job is the hero, and the God of creation is the monster. In the end, it is the creator God that has a kind of unconsciousness to him. He does not see, or refuses to see, what his actions have done to Job. All the restoration in the world does not make it right, even though God seems to think that it does. In the Book of Revelation when God wipes away all the tears, does he also wipe away all the horrible memories? Does the end justify the means? The highest part of us abhors that kind of thinking as violence against honest love. As in the Book of Job, we find ourselves being bigger than the God we say is so vast.

Our ability to judge the created order is a result of our having eaten from the Tree of Knowledge - that is the metaphor. Within our consciousness of self and the world, the deficiency becomes obvious to us. The God of the garden hunts us. We become aware of our nakedness - our vulnerability. This is the first key to understanding ourselves. We become mindful of our own suffering, and no matter what we do or try to do, our suffering remains. Why? As the Buddha said, "Life is suffering". And let us be clear about this, even if we as human beings were morally perfect - life itself would still be suffering. Our morality, or lack thereof, is not the ultimate cause of suffering itself. To be sure, our hurtful actions increase the intense suffering that we already feel. We trap ourselves all the more in a kind of secondary reality that becomes just another layer of the material reality that terrorizes us. In essence, "we become what we hate," as an old Jewish proverb asserts. Which is why Jesus would say that loving your enemy is the only way to spiritual efficiency. Our social systems begin to look like the very thing that scares us the most. Perhaps the first Gnostic principle should be, "Be aware - and stay awake." In other words, know what you're dealing with, and don't make it worse.

In Gnosticism the recognition is that the world is necessarily evil, because is just not enough. It is deficient as the raw material, so to speak, to fulfill our spiritual needs. There is more inside than there is outside. As The Gospel of Thomas (vs. 56 - The Nag Hammadi Library) puts it: "Whoever has come to understand the world has found only a corpse, and whoever has found a corpse is superior to the world." Part of the point is, to turn away from ascribing ultimacy to the world in any fashion.

Within our own psychology we understand that frequently we create whole world views and attitudes out of a single aspect of ourselves. That is to say, we create a reality set out of a single feature of our feelings or our personality. The difficulty for a depressed person, for instance, is that their entire world becomes an aspect of their depression. In a manner of speaking, they create an entire world from a single aspect of themselves, and not from the entirety of their personhood. In fact, the state of depression can even become a kind of mind unto itself - blocking everything else from getting through. In this way, the Gnostics are saying, human beings are like mini-universes, or a microcosm.

The same is true for the created order. It lacks a kind of fullness, and has come forth from a particular feature of the entirety - not the entirety itself. Although the world in some fashion can have no life at all without some of the entirety, it does not reflect the entirety of all spirituality. It is deficient. We feel this deficiency in everything we do in this world. This deficiency causes the suffering. The deficiency is like a great sleeping potion, and awakening from its hold is required before one can see the deficiency at all.

The metaphysical problem of how a loving God could possibly create something as deficient as this material world, imbued with mindless process, is the subject of Gnostic myth. Usually the myths revolve around "emanations" which come from Depth and Silence (The Father and Mother of the entirety called the Pleroma). These entities come forth in pairs, which in turn then emanate aspects of their being into other pairs. Generally these emanations, or Aeons are numbered at thirty. There are many good scholarly works on this subject. At some point, the myths explain that the last of the Aeons - Sophia (Wisdom), desired to break through and know the fullness of Depth and Silence—making an attempt to do so without the aid of the entirety. This attempt created suffering - which the Valentinian Gnostic documents say became "dense like a fog" (The Gospel of Truth ). It is within this dense suffering that Sophia gives birth to the creator God—who because of the denseness of the fog, does not realize that he is not alone, nor is he the only god. He then creates the material world based upon a reflection of the spiritual order he sees against the backdrop of the fog. Since the world is built upon merely a reflection, and is designed out of ignorance, it becomes deficient, or as The Gospel of Truth puts it: error.

Gnostic myths paint a picture into a deeper truth that cannot be spoken of directly, only pointed to. This is the nature of all real spiritual truth. The point of the myths is that the world comes forth from features of the spiritual that lack fullness - much like what we as humans do when we create an attitude or reality set out of a single feature within our own personality. And because this creation, although deficient, comes forth ultimately from the entirety - evil is only indirectly ascribed to it, as we awaken to its emptiness. Human Beings, who have some residue from the "All", and therefore a "spark" of that uncreated light beyond the created world, are sent a messenger to awaken them to the reality of their "True Self"— That which is divine, and not a product of the deficiency. Thus the world is suffering and Human Beings feel the intensity of that suffering because something inside of them is greater than the world.

## Recommended Reading

*"While his wisdom contemplates the Word, and his teaching utters it, his knowledge has revealed it."*

-The Gospel of Truth

## Gnostic Scriptures

Hans-Joachim Klimkeit, Gnosis on the Silk Road: Gnostic Texts from Central Asia (San Francisco: Harper, 1993).

Bentley Layton, The Gnostic Scriptures (Garden City, NY: Doubleday & Co., 1987).

Marvin Meyer, The Gospel of Thomas: The Hidden Sayings of Jesus (Harper San Francisco, 1992).

Marvin Meyer, The Secret Teachings of Jesus: Four Gnostic Gospels (New York: Random House, 1984.)

James Robinson, ed., The Nag Hammadi Library in English (New York: Harper & Row, 1977; revised edition, San Francisco: Harper, 1988)

Some Gnostic Books for your Library

Giovanni Filoramo, A History of Gnosticism (Oxford and Cambridge, Mass.: Basil Blackwell, 1990).

Stephan Hoeller, Jung and the Lost Gospels: Insights into the Dead Sea Scrolls and the Nag Hammadi Library (Wheaton, Il.: Quest Books, 1989).

Stuart Holroyd, The Elements of Gnosticism, (Shaftesbury, Dorset, England and Rockport, MA: Element Books, 1994.)

Hans Jonas, The Gnostic Religion: The Message of the Alien God (Boston: Beacon, 1963).

Elaine Pagels, The Gnostic Gospels (New York: Random House, 1978).

Elaine Pagels, Adam, Eve and the Serpent (New York: Random House, 1988).

Simone Petrement, A Separate God: The Christian Origins of Gnosticism (San Francisco: Harper, 1990).

Kurt Rudolph, Gnosis: The Nature and History of Gnosticism (San Francisco, Harper & Row, 1983).

Christan D. Amundsen, Insights from the Secret Teachings of Jesus: The Gospel of Thomas (Sunstar, Fairfield, Iowa, 1998).

# A Few Key Gnostic Words

The following is a brief list of commonly used Gnostic words. It is by no means exhaustive and complete. These few words are words that anyone who wishes to begin the journey into Gnostic truth needs to have command of and use with respect.

Adam – When the creator God fashioned man from earth, he made him from a shadow image cast from the light of spiritual reality beyond his knowledge. Thus, his Adam was comprised of only physical and mental capabilities, but lacked spirit. There are various accounts of how the sprit became involved with the earthly Adam. Either out of compassion for the creators mistaken ability to fashion true life, or as an act of being captured by the powers of darkness, the sprit fell into the earthly Adam. This spiritual Adam or Man of Light that fell into the earthly Adam – is a divine being, who is not created by the Demiurge, but is the real essence of life within the earthly Adam. The awakening of this spiritual Adam is the centerpiece of gnosis, since life in the body is a kind of heaviness that puts the spirit to sleep or into an intoxicated state. Often times the figure of Adam is viewed as a metaphor for the soul which is in need of awakening through the work of the spirit, which is understood as Eve.

Acquaintance – intimate knowledge and experience of the divine presence as a spark within. The essence of gnosis.

Aeon – emanated aspects of the divine reality, usually understood as pairs (male and female) that balance one another. Depth-Silence (the original pair of Aeons) emanates mind-Truth, etc. The Aeons make up the world of spiritual reality called the "Fullness" or Pleroma.

Alien (or the Spirit) – The Spark of divine reality present within us and in life as it is animated. It is uncreated, and its source of being resides outside the universe of material and energy forms.

**Alienation** – The inner sense of feeling lost within something that is foreign and totally other. Forlorn and homesick. Alienation is the source of anxiety, fear and other negative emotions such as anger and frustration.

**Archons** – Created angels of the Demiurge or powers of the world, which keep the spirit locked into place and asleep to the truth of its own reality.

**Christ** – The Christ is understood to be a separate spiritual reality or aeon than is the historical figure of Jesus. The Christ came upon Jesus and walked in the world through him as the revealer of the alien God and the transcendent reality. The Christ is said to have left Jesus at the time of his death on the cross, where Jesus said: "My God, My God, why have you forsaken me?" The work of the Christ is as a revealer/redeemer figure – that awakens the Gnostic to the saving gnosis, or knowledge of true self. The Christ is also said to await our spirit's return to the "fullness," where he opens the door between the worlds of darkness and light.

**Cosmos (Universe)** – The material world, which is termed ignorance or error, and is seen as the world of darkness, and the realm of being lost. More existentially understood it is termed a blind process, or the "hardened stuff" of alienation. Sometimes the cosmos or universe is seen as evil, but more often than not simply deficient of spiritual presence, and lacking in fullness – devoid of meaning in and of itself; empty.

**Darkness** – Generally understood as the material world or the cosmos. Darkness is also another word for ignorance or blindness, and thus the spirit is said to be living in darkness in the world both metaphorically and literally.

**Demiurge (Creator God)** – Literally the creator of the universe, or fashioner of the material world. Usually seen as the aborted child of Sophia, a divine aeon who in her desire to know the totality of the fullness, caused great grief and suffering which was cast away from the fullness of Spiritual Reality, and fashioned into the material world by her son – Ialdabaoth, the blind God. Sometimes in Gnosticism, this God is identified as the God of the Jewish Bible Yahweh.

Emanation – birthed aspects of the divine original pair Depth & Silence. Emanation is not creation, which is an objectification and fashioning of something from the outside with material. Emanation is the imparting of qualities of self from one divine aspect into another through the extension of light. For Example: Our true self is emanated, while our material and psychic selves are created and fashioned through the material process of the world.

Eve – The Genesis story of Adam and Eve is never seen as literal history in Gnosticism, but as myth with a deep intrapsychic meaning. The figure of Eve is generally seen as representing the spirit, and is given a place of honor in Gnostic thinking. Eve awakens Adam who is asleep to his spiritual essence, where he realizes that he is greater than the god who created him. The drama of this myth continues when Adam is put to sleep and in his sleep is told that Eve is created out of his rib, which is a lie meant to enslave Eve under the domination of the demi-urge. The feminine aspect of the divine reality has a place of great significance in Gnosticism, since it is the quality that awakens the hardness of the sleeping soul.

Fall – The idea of the fall is symbolic of the pre-cosmic movement of a spark of the divine into the world of matter. The spirit, or spark is seen as falling down into darkness, and then captured or held by that darkness.

Fullness – The spiritual reality beyond the mundane world. Also called Pleroma, this spiritual reality is the true source of all being. Since the material world is often referred to as emptiness, the spiritual world is therefore referred to as fullness.

**Gnosis** – The Greek word for knowledge or acquaintance, which in this sense has a saving characteristic to it – knowledge of one's true self, the divine spark or spirit. Gnosis is saving in that it begins the true journey home from the material world of shadow, to the spirit world of light. This journey home is seen both metaphorically and figuratively, as well as literally – that the spirit has fallen into darkness, and must awaken to its true identity before that journey can take place.

**Gnostics** – Those who have awakened. It is said in Gnosticism that the spirit feels homesick, which is also the root cause of alienation, dread and being forlorn.

**Lost** – This word, which is akin to homesick and alienation, is the most fundamental state of the spirit – lost in a strange and alien world. The condition of being lost creates in the spirit its sleep or intoxication, and it is from this lostness that awakening to the truth of one's real origin that begins the journey home. This journey home is, like most Gnostic concepts, seen both metaphorically and literally. The spirit is lost within and without – it has lost its sense of self, and is lost amidst an alien world of concrete form that is a shadow world.

**Morality** – Gnostics do not see morality as salvific in nature. Although how one behaves and orients oneself in the world is important, it is not the critical issue --which is knowledge of one's true self. One must hasten to say, that while morality is not salvific in the strictest sense, it is also a reflection of one's inner knowledge. To behave towards others in a destructive and hurtful way denotes ignorance of self and others. Gnostics are called upon to search deeply within themselves for the essential path to follow, since all external laws are only shadows.

**Pearl** – Generally speaking this is a Ghostic metaphor for the spirit. Refernces to the pearl are all through Gnostic literature, and central to The Hymn of the Pearl – a beautiful Gnostic poetic piece about the "saved savior".

Pleroma – The fullness of the unknown God, which includes all the abstract qualities of the divine "personality." The Pleroma is also referred to as the world of light, as opposed to the darkness of the "created world."

Pneumatic(s) – the Greek word for spirit. Pneumatics then, are spiritual people, or Gnostics.

Psychics – This generally refers to "ordinary" religious people, who have not reached a level of awakening, but stand somewhere in between pneumatic and those that are strictly involved with the material (hylic). The psychics are the "ignorant ones" who are blind to the truth of themselves, and are wrapped up with their own psychology, and haven't worked beyond their false sense of self. These people tend to mistake the false creation for ultimate reality.

Spark – The spirit is referred to as a spark. A "piece" of the divine light that has fallen from the fullness into the dark world of material creation.

Sophia – A feminine aspect of the Plemora or Fullness of God identified as "wisdom." It is from Sophia's suffering and desire that the material world is formed, and her involvement in the awakening of the fallen sparks is seen as critical.

Soul – The soul is viewed differently than the spirit in Gnostic thought. The soul is a created part of the earthly person, which is the place of mental and emotional attributes. The spirit awakens the soul to consciousness of the spirit within, and begins the process of loosening the hold of mental and emotional traps that keep the spirit enslaved to the world of darkness and emptiness. In the Genesis story, the figure of Adam is generally viewed as a metaphor for the soul.